THE DIARY OF

OSHUN

The Diary of Oshun

Written By
Valencia Marie

Copyright © 2022 Indulgent Insights

All rights reserved. No part of this book may be used or reproduced in any manner whatsoever without the written permission of the author or publisher. Printed in the United States of America.

Marie, Valencia

    The Diary of Oshun

ISBN: 978-1-7376226-3-5

First Edition

DEDICATION

Intrinsically, there must be a page of dedication, or acknowledgment when writing a book. This, by far, has been the most difficult part. Not because I don't have anyone to thank; it's quite the opposite, actually.

There are so many women, who I've listened to throughout the years, who deserve to be acknowledged.

Whether it be a stranger who feels they can share their life experiences with me, or an old friend needing an ear or counsel.

A family member expressing teachings in an attempt to aid us through a life of not experiencing the same mistakes they've made or a kid who is silently trying not to be noticed in order to find out all the juicy stories narrated by aunts, grandmothers and cousins.

This story is dedicated to all of us.

The ones who have stories but are unable to tell them.

Who have stories to tell but feel they aren't being listened to.

And the ones who are just finding their voice. Our stories transcend history books. They keep our traditions alive, keep us alive.

I love you all, thank you.

…Also, I have to thank my Monkey, my Doodie, my Mini Me, my daughter. Your strength is immeasurable. Your love is indescribable. I am so proud of the woman you've become and you still "wow" me every day.
You are my person, Sonja.
I love you.

TABLE OF CONTENTS

Introduction

Reprimand……………………………………….. 3

The Moon………………………………………… 4

Indebted…………………………………………..6

Everything………………………………………..7

Eyes………………………………………………...8

Wet Verses………………………………………..9

The Walk Out…..………………………………..11

Nikki Giovanni, Sweet Lies Bitter Truth………..12

Conversation…………………………………….17

Whirlwind……………………………..………….18

A Soul's Affair …………………………………. 20

Ooohhh…………………………………………. 21

Let Me See………………………………………. 22

Stages…………………………………………….. 23

Perception………………………………………. 24

Fisherman……………………………………….. 25

"cum dumpster"……………………………….. 27

Text Message with a Direct Message ………… 31

Tricked …………………………………………..34

Smitten..35

Entry 5,271... 36

Patience Patients.............................. 38

Moods... 45

The Forbidden.. 47

Oshun's Karma.. 49

My Head..51

My Heart.. 51

My Hope... 51

Shadow Work...52

DNA..55

Danger.. 56

Hey! Real Quick..................................... 57

INTRODUCTION

Ō-SHūN

Is said to be the Goddess of fertility, growth, love, lust.
She is among the most beautiful of the Orisha and also possesses human attributes.
If wronged, if abused, if hurt… Oshun can be vengeful, spiteful, insatiable in her lust to punish those who wrong her.
Often called vain, I call her misunderstood. Would one call a beautiful flower vain for believing it so?
Oshun embodies, in part, all women.
The following is a small glimpse into her diary:
Accounts of Oshun inside our mortal bodies and our experiences.
We are majestic as a goddess is.
We contain unwavering strength as the waters she commands. An insurmountable loyalty to those we love.
And an unquestionable desire to BE loved.

REPRIMAND

Don't be petulant.
I am not one of these women that doesn't realize when someone is trying to manage and manipulate a conversation
I have not nor will I ever disrespect you
And would you like to know why?
Because I promised I wouldn't
Also, don't fucking threaten me with not speaking to me for the rest of the day, like you are punishing me
You don't want to play the dictator in this "situation ship"
Don't take for granted that I feel a certain way for you
Don't be a tyrant and don't be malicious to someone who doesn't deserve it,
just because you've been through shit
Stop testing me
I AM YOUR QUEEN

THE MOON

Does my femininity strike you as fragility?
I am a Goddess who's portrayed by the world as
being at the bottom of the totem pole
You other races and genders
Could never play our role
Or take our role,
Get it?
I'm so tired of having to be so damn specific
You niggas act like you don't really get it
Better yet, you see our magnificence
but won't admit it
You pay us less
You make us stress
So we wear less
Trying to impress
The people who couldn't care less
About our happiness
What does it do for you?
To tear us down the way you do

Without a care or even a clue
Of how our mere existence benefits you
I see the condescension
I see what you could never have done
I had your children
I raised your sons
I taught them compassion
You beat them and told them I was wrong
I cooked your food
I strengthened your mood
And when you needed love
I satiated that too
There could be no life without the Moon
There would be no life without the Black Woman in you

INDEBTED

Your face invited me
Your eyes pierced me
Your lips called to me
Your voice touched me
Your smile affected me
Thank you

EVERYTHING

You are...

Black

A beautiful, edible, insatiable black

A black I want to melt into and hide away from

A black that say

I come from you and we are one

Your eyes pierce me

Devour me

Your mouth calls my name and entrances me

I can't stop looking at you

EYES

My eyes?
And what of my mouth?
My smile, my skin
My nose, my cheeks and chin?
I want you to worship all of it
Gaze at all of it
Taste all of it
Stare down at me in wonder
Watch me cum while choking me and staring into the gates of my soul
Feel me clinch tight
Seizing your majesty as you also come to the brink
Call my name with those captivating lips
Feel every sensation
But don't you dare take your eyes off of me

WET VERSES

Should've worn panties
Under this dress, wet
Turn to the side
So I don't get my couch, wet
Squeezing really tight
Because I'm tingling, wet
Needing you
Deep inside of me, wet
On top
Because I need all of you, wet
Slip, slide, glide,
and grinding you, wet
Take my time
There's no place I'd rather be, wet
No precursors or foreplay
We can do that later, bet
Just let me hold you, show you
What this pussy do, wet
Pick up the pace

You stay in place don't need your help, yet
Just watch me but don't stop me
I'm about to cum, then
Hot spillage from your village
Cascade on my chest
Lay back now
Relax now
Let me suck out the rest

THE WALK OUT

Why would you do that to me?
Why would you let me share my poetry?
Why spend the energy telling me what we could be
If all you really wanted to do was fuck me
What kind of person must you be
Someone who sets out to deceive
Someone beautiful inside and out such as me
You must be so unhappy
I wish the best for you.
I wish I could have loved you
Because you really need it, you do
Someone must have really hurt you
Tortured cyclical you

NIKKI GIOVANNI, SWEET LIES BITTER TRUTHS

Lie to me

Don't give me attitude

Your angry looks

Your solemn mood

Depression is the expression

As you learn life's lessons

Da Man you tried impressin

Has you feeling pressed in

Lie to me

You aren't the only one with a hard day

Schedules and meetings don't go your way

Boss is always asking me to stay

But I have to pick up Baby J

And my period is late

God my period is late

Lie to me

When we come home

Both feeling stressed and alone

Lay down that somber tone

This is where we belong
Though negativity from the day is strong
And this world treats you wrong
Show me a smile sing me a song
Whisper sweet nothings all night long
The world outside should not get the best of you
They don't cook, clean, and put it down for you
They don't nurture your dreams and provide for you
They don't love you, my King, I do
So lie to me if you have to

OFTEN CALLED VAIN, I CALL HER

MISUNDERSTOOD

CONVERSATION

Full of emotion, full of life, full of untapped approval.
You don't know what it means
when you tell me you want me.
That you like who and what I am, as I am.
You have no idea what your words and positive
proclamations do to a tortured soul like mine.
I am in awe of how you know what I am feeling.
I love that you smile incessantly when we see each
other.
I'm even moved when you get frustrated with me
after a misunderstanding.
Because I see you.
I know what that means.
I know it's because you care, that I can strike a chord
with you so quickly.
You are a treasure to me.
I'm happy to have met you.
You make me stronger.

WHIRLWIND

I'm beautiful

And You want me

I'm beautiful

But you'll hurt me

I've had an overdue realization

While you fantasize about the sensation

Try to characterize the relation

While my heart and soul is being caved in

Now I'm a *goal* digger

I will not tiptoe around your hurt feelings

My intuition tells me you mean harm

She is NEVER wrong

She is the reason I'm strong

Obviously… honestly

You cannot afford me

Can't afford my energy

My time

My efforts

My abilities

(Because I'm damn near magical)

…And you surely can't afford this tongue

This hip

This air

This lip

These words that only a Goddess can possess

I wield them

I strike with them

I cause your unrest

A SOUL'S AFFAIR

How did I find you?
The more we converse the more I know
this is no coincidence
The more I look at you the more I realize it is
something larger speaking to me
Telling me this man in some way is connected to me
A being that rivals yet matches my own
I've found in his gaze a home
And for once I don't want to be alone
Wrap me in your warm embrace
Fingers interlaced
Soft lips caress my face
Space and time could never replace
Such an unheard of protected place
But you're married...

OOOHHH

Ooohhh if I were with you
Celebrating we would do
I'd lick the tip
Stop
Then sit on you
Ride it
Get up
Then suck my juice off you
Ooohhh…

LET ME SEE

The winter is cold
So is your soul
You're really ok with this road
On which you choose to go
You are hurting me so
I don't want to let go
Please
Don't let me go
Just let me see your face
Let me get a taste
Of what it's like to look into your eyes
If not I'll be forced to surmise
That all you want to do is hide
And therefore can never be mine

STAGES

What do you think about the company I keep
The pictures I send and the approval I seek
Hours we've spent in the last few days
Getting acquainted learning each other's ways
Timid with our dealings invading each other's space
Would love to mount, straddle, kiss your chocolate face
It's early but I'm not interested in casual fun
Though our energies and synergies suggest you're the one
Time reveal if what we feel will lead us to share the same space
With whispered moans, arched backs and fingers interlaced…
Damn…

PERCEPTION

I like looking at you
And I like looking at the way you look at me
It's both excited and serene
The creases at the corners of your eyes
Increase the warmth and wetness between my thighs
How can a look physically touch me as yours does
Why does the curve of your lips feel like a hug
Did you cast a spell
Because I know full well
That this isn't me
I am confident and composed
As a real Goddess should be
But I feel my palace crumble every time I see
Those patient hooded eyes staring through me
That dark chocolate skin waiting to be
Tasted and caressed as a wave folds into the sea
I would give my immortality to be with thee

FISHERMAN

Just imagine falling for someone you've never seen
The mere thought of it just seems so obscene
Someone who caresses your thoughts
and snuggles your dreams
Who believes who you are even when you don't
believe
One who knows your fears
but also understands what they mean
Who cares for you despite your damaged being
He's patient and kind
But only a dream
Callous and cruel for continuing to be
The perfect match the one for me
I see through the spell so vividly
Why do I have to beg to spend time with you
Are you not really you
Are you my masked savior
A voice I have come to need but can never see
You've created a trigger inside of me
What do you have to hide

Are the feelings only on one side
You've become the link to whether I live or die
I knew from the beginning you were a lie
But you made me feel so good inside
You build scenarios off of my shit
Or regurgitate scenes off of fake TV hits
I love you still though I admit
That the only explanation is that I'm being cat-fished

"cum dumpster"

Let me guess…

I'm a slut

I'm a hoe

I'm a freak

Got a different dick everyday of the week

Repeated like a repetitious, classic written, hip hop track

Just enough to make me want to slam my head

But not enough to push me over the edge

Just enough to find me sitting in a dark closet rocking

But not enough to have the paramedics knocking

Just enough to silently cut my arms and legs

But not enough for me to end it… instead

Tell me again how I ruined your life

How you could have had such a better wife

How my rape and abuse was possibly wanted

How promiscuity was all I really wanted

The shackles of my love afforded me truths

Of how hurt people, hurt people

even the ones who claim to love you
Thank you for being who I needed you to be
Thank you for constantly saying
I tricked you into marrying me
Thank you so much for beating me without raising a fist
Thank you for after showering me with hate wanting
to end it with a sadistic loving kiss
For leaving me every other weekend for 5 years
For taking pride that every time it led me to tears
I couldn't understand why you'd want to stay
with such a monster
Why you wouldn't end it, leave her, divorce her
It's because you got joy from torturing her
You felt vindicated when you'd make her suffer
My protector, my lover, my rescuer…
Is an imposter

Your loving ex-wife,
AKA "cum dumpster"

WOULD ONE CALL A BEAUTIFUL FLOWER VAIN FOR BELIEVING IT SO?

TEXT MESSAGE WITH A DIRECT MESSAGE

White him say:
I'm curious about all the rumors pertaining to a black woman. You know, "once you go black you never go back." They ride better than anyone. Outstanding bedroom game. Fuller lips. Better kissers. You know, the usual stuff.

Black her say:
It's quite curious that everything you're curious about black women pertains to sex.

White him say:
Going off of things I heard. I would say women have a lot of the same qualities and myths regardless of skin color.

Black her say:
What about the fact that we're stronger, more resilient, more loyal, more dedicated to our men?

Because we HAVE to be. Because an average kind of love is not enough to sustain our men and what they encounter from the world on a day to day basis.

White him say:
I think those qualities can be related to any woman, if she is a great woman and knows what she wants.

Black her say:
(Begins dictation) So this is too much to type… What you're telling me is that you wonder if we ride better than anyone, our bedroom game is outstanding. Better kissers, fuller lips, once you go black you never go back… the usual stuff, you say.
But, it's not possible for us to also be more strong, or more resilient, or more loyal, or more loving, or more dedicated to our men???
So we can be better sexually, but not in any other aspect of our being, huh?
I'm… I'm just trying to understand…

White him say:
 No, I just mean that ALL women are capable of loving harder and caring more… Was I out of line?

Black her say:
No, it's cool… But I will tell you this… I don't just ride better…
I can spell my name in cursive with my hips
I'd have you reaching blindly to grip
My bedroom strategies are classic
Tactics are matchless
Trying to find your way around my body
you'll need an atlas
Hydrate Sweetie, your sweat is all over the mattress.

TRICKED

You...
You were starting to make me like you
Enjoy your ideas your goodness your time too
The rise the fall of your breathing
Like the tide as it swells then receding
You...
You were starting to make me like you
Your confident comforting air
Assurities you wanted to be here
Was it my actions that made you disappear
No call or text maybe I'm too square (LOL)
No words from you but posts on social media-sphere
I've done nothing wrong
"Block game strong"
I remember…

SMITTEN

Careful staring into me with those eyes.
Fragile is the woman you're staring into.
How dare you understand the inner workings of my mind.
Remind me of what it feels like to be consumed by someone's gaze.
So quiet, yet so telling forcing me to look away.
I'm smitten.

ENTRY 5,271

Forgive... yes forgive

But don't forget what these muthafucka's did to you

Don't forget how much you suffered

How much pain was caused

and how under appreciated you were

You deserve the WORLD

Go out and get that shit!

All of them don't want to hurt you

Talk down to you

Disrespect and belittle you

There are those who want to uplift, support, love, comfort, and uphold you

With the belief that the two of you can accomplish anything

Don't let him call you a hoe

Don't let him tell you, you bring nothing to the table

You are the muthafuckin table

Don't allow him to tell you that you aren't attractive

You are the creator of all things

There is no life without you
Your blackness and womanly ways
Provide a beautiful immortal shade
You're not a hoe
You bring plenty
And you are a beautiful black woman

PATIENCE PATIENTS

I remember in my youth,
Still filled with hope beautiful truths
I dreamed of how things would come to be
Like getting straight A's and getting a degree
Or going on stage captivating them when I sing
But there was one thing which I wanted best
One that I dreamed of more than the rest
It was to be found by my perfect black prince
For him to shield me and love me simply because I exist
To love me and hold me and live utter bliss
We'd have a house full of children and a white picket fence
Such dreams would shatter when I turned eleven
Older men of family friends would touch my body cause I don't matter

My brand new budding breast slightly poking through my shirt
Soft peach fuzz hair on what I would futurely relate to as Hurt
Slender waist curves into hips that look amazing in my pleated skirt
Hair in a fancy French braid on the side really cute
Baby hairs brushed out and slid down curly q's
Later that night I'd be taking cues
From men under the guise of drunkenness coming into the room
Reaching under striped pjs that me and my friend thought were cool
Feeling a guilty chill from a feeling that
I didn't learn in school
It electrifies your young new body and you don't know what to do
I cry and lay still while he has the nerve to sing a tune
Not forgetting to caress my budding breast, squeezing new nipples too
I gotta figure out how I can be
Build a sensual callous wall around myself tenderly

And show these men what they can really get
Cause telling daddy would only get him and my uncles hit
With life time sentences from getting this nigga hit
Taking him to Lake Maggorie everybody gets a hit
With baseball bats and other inanimate household shit
Taking his battered body and throwing it in a ditch
Lead bait for the gators to come finish off this bitch
But no that's selfish and I need my family here
So I weaponize the pussy
My mind thinking I have them entranced by my stare
My slight seductive twelve-year-old smile
knows what's in the air
It's my pussy, grown nigga feast your eyes on this derriere
Watch my hips sway as I walk in the room
Of this childhood water party
bathing suite new
I squat and I bend to give him a view
Tiny beads of water all over me too
I swing my summer braids I can tell he's about to lose

His sanity in this litany of kid food and booze
He's staring so hard he doesn't care who's there
He leads me away from the party and stares
My beauty, he tells me, moves him to tears
Can he please show me something that'll feel so good
Better than cupcakes and Christmas breaks and even birthdays to?
I'm just going to take this toy out of my pants
and give it all to you
Promise not to make a sound or the fun will end for you
Then all your family and friends will no longer like you
All because you didn't make me feel good in this room
He stripped off the bottom of his clothing and pushed my beautiful brand new bathing suit aside
Then stabbed me with a blinding pain that hurt deep inside
He pushed, grunted, and stroked my hair
I cried and cried and cried
He doesn't care that he's hurting me

he's pushing harder still

Grunting down at me with lust in his eye

He's going faster and harder still

I'm getting scratched from leaves and

branches below as he goes faster and harder still

My brand new pussy throbs and aches as he shudders

and then lays still

My hair is matted, innocence gone and yet he lays on

me still

I look around me, reach for the ruggedly torn bottle

Now he'll forever lay still...

OSHUN EMBODIES, IN PART, ALL WOMEN

MOODS

I can tell

I can tell your moods

Upbeat moods

Serious moods

Mr. Gray moods

Sensual moods

I can tell the mood you are in

when you're thinking about me

The mood you're in when thinking what could be

My moods?

I have a mood that's lovely

A mood that steals

A mood that helps

And a mood that heals

I have a mood so blue it'll tear your heart in two

But also there's a mood when I think of you

It holds me, restores me

It lifts me up too

With my mood I feel this presence in you

One that's gentle and kind and wants more of me too
What am I going to do with you
You make love to my mind
Its sensual yet true
"Please don't hurt me"
Is all I ask of you

THE FORBIDDEN

There are literally 20 people that I could be talking to…
But I can only seem to think of you
I don't want to hear anyone else's voice
Or their word choice
Or the timbre
Or their vernacular
I don't want to see anyone else's face
Or imagine how anyone else lips taste
Or look at another's seductive stare
Or how when they want me, their nostrils flare
From the carnal desire of wanting me…
But alas, I can't
I shan't
Take you from the ~~current bondage, contract~~,
I mean marriage that you are confined to,
you're not aligned to
Nor designed to
Be in a relationship that doesn't stir your soul

Force forgotten parts of you to lose control
The fear of a cardinal sin
Does not outweigh the fear of not speaking to me
again…
So I'll wait
For a time at least
I'll wait

OSHUN'S KARMA

I'm not going to cheat
Because that would be lowering myself
And quite frankly my beautiful, psychedelic,
magical love cave
Is life altering and not to be given away just to get
even
I would leave
But first, I would show him
how my love has magnified his life
I would pay all the bills for the month
I would cook his favorite dinner
wearing heels and nothing else
I would sing to him while he ate
Tantalizing him with soft kisses
I'd lead him to the shower and bathe every inch of
him
With extreme attention to detail

Then…

I would fuck him to tears

And then again to sleep

…Finally, while he's resting with a hint of a smile on

his lips

I'd take a picture and silently leave

Then I'd text him the picture

With a message saying

YOU will NEVER be that happy again…

MY HEAD

You are a work of art

Which shade is not yet on the color chart

While I exhibit your magnificence

I analyze and determine that your color does not yet exist

This new hue is now a part of me

And everywhere I look it's what I see

Naturally I'm drawn to thee

MY HEART

It hurts

But I'm learning

And I won't wait for you

Be what I need you to be

Or… don't… be

MY HOPE …

SHADOW WORK

I was young

I was abused

Oversexualized

Confused

Five times I had fetuses ripped from my womb

Not pregnancies from rape but from being consumed

With making random men feel good by any means

Even if that meant allowing them

the pleasure to release inside me

I grew up got married to a man who'd say I wasn't

worthy

Because when I was young, time and time again

I chose to be other men's trophies

There was a sick twisted need for their attention

So when a man finally loved me

I purposely failed to mention

I wanted so bad to have more children.

I adored being a mother to the one I was given

He denied me for years

because he didn't want someone like me to carry his lineage

How could he explain to future children

what their mother really is

A cumdumpster

A sex monster

She was born to be this way

"Sexual abuse doesn't result in women being whores",

he'd say

I fed him truth pieces

I begged and I pleaded

Then finally conceded

This isn't what we needed

Now I'm back to my maiden name

I'm alone, his hatred treatment ingrained

Lived a remnant of life circling the drain

Trudging out of the muck of heartache and shame

Epic memories implosion of histories tied to one name

Shadow work is supposed to bring pain

Working through issues, snot and tear stained tissues

Healed healthy love for myself is what I will gain

DNA

I want to be interlaced like when your braids… are braided
Like all the breaths of smoke
you created when you get faded
Interlaced like our thoughts on the same frequency
Like the synergetic heat I can feel coming from you
and you feel coming from me
Even deeper… like the DNA strands inside of me
A double helix are we

DANGER

My words can slice like a Hattori Hanzō sword
But instead I breathlessly hold them
like a Phoenix feather on an open palm
praying for once that no breeze comes through
Rage can only be checked for so long
Rage can be replayed like a song
And after allowing it to build and build as one would
edging towards climax
I explode!
An unpressurized blast of the results from built up
despair, heartache, and abuse
A mushroom cloud of belittlement, depression and
anxiety
And finally the fallout of mistrust, bitter treatment,
and a hint of cyclical psychotic behaviors

HEY! REAL QUICK...

I must be still healing

Because I caught myself trying to convince You

that you should spend time with ME

And that's a mistake, I mean that cannot be

Because I am the prize

It is a privilege to bask in the glow of my scene

AND AN UNQUESTIONABLE DESIRE

TO BE LOVED

www.ingramcontent.com/pod-product-compliance
Lightning Source LLC
Chambersburg PA
CBHW030916080526
44589CB00010B/328